A
BOOK
OF
POSTCARDS
OF
30
HISTORICAL
PHOTOGRAPHS

IRELAND 1900

POMEGRANATE ARTBOOKS, SAN FRANCISCO

Pomegranate Artbooks
Box 808022
Petaluma, CA 94975

Pomegranate publishes several other postcard collections of historical photographs of major cities in the world, including London, New York and San Francisco. Please write to the publisher for more information.

Designed by Katie Burke

Printed in Korea

The photographs in this collection were taken in the period around 1900, from about 1880 to the early 1920s. They portray the land and people of Ireland, a country whose way of life has changed very little since the time of these pictures. Through these images, Ireland emerges as a country of contrasts. It is a place of craggy, rocky cliffs and soft rolling hills; of rough seas and gentle mists. Despite a history of hardship and strife, its people display a quiet dignity and strength.

Stone walls, thatched cottages, castles, peat bogs, fishing boats, rivers and bays — these timeless features have for centuries enthralled Ireland's visitors and inspired her artists and writers. They are evident here in this collection's country portraits. Also featured are vintage scenes of Ireland's towns and Dublin, the bustling capital city whose name "Dubh Linn" meant "dark pool" in reference to the peat-colored waters of its River Liffey.

Many events in Ireland's turbulent history were enacted in Dublin. Its main thoroughfare, O'Connell Street (formerly Sackville Street), was named in honor of the statesman Daniel O'Connell (1775–1847), who secured Catholic Emancipation in 1829. The General Post Office was the site of the 1916 Easter Rising, which eventually led to the formation of the Republic of Ireland in 1921. Across from the post office stood the statue of Lord Nelson, known as Nelson's Pillar, until the IRA blew it up in 1966.

For a country of her size, Ireland has produced a disporportionately large number of writers who constitute some of the greatest in the English language: Oliver Goldsmith (1730–74), Oscar Wilde (1854–1900), William Butler Yeats (1865–1939), George Bernard Shaw (1856–1950),

John Millington Synge (1817–1909), James Joyce (1882–1941), Sean O'Casey (1884–1964) and Samuel Beckett (1906–1989). What other country so highly esteems its literary heritage that it erects a statue in memory of one of its favorite story tellers, Galway's Padraig O'Conaire (1882–1923)?

This album of rare photographs evokes the rich heritage and beauty of Ireland. it is a poignant journey for the millions of Americans who trace their ancestry back to Ireland, as well as for everyone who shares a fascination for this magnificent country.

IRELAND 1900

County Tipperary. The Rock of Cashel, where Irish kings were crowned and the last king of Munster is buried.

POMEGRANATE • BOX 808022 • PETALUMA, CA 94975

IRELAND 1900

Trinity College, Dublin, founded by Elizabeth I in 1591. The classical facade pictured here was constructed between 1755 and 1759.

POMEGRANATE • BOX 808022 • PETALUMA, CA 94975

IRELAND 1900
Bantry Bay, County Cork. The town of Bantry lies at the end of the Bay.

POMEGRANATE • BOX 808022 • PETALUMA, CA 94975

IMBER RON LATES RICKS EMENT
MPLEMENTS&

IRELAND 1900
County of Limerick. A farmer holds up his pig for inspection by prospective buyers.

POMEGRANATE • BOX 808022 • PETALUMA, CA 94975

IRELAND 1900
Peasant huts in Connemara

POMEGRANATE • BOX 808022 • PETALUMA, CA 94975

IRELAND 1900
Enniskillen, County Fermanagh (viewed from the south)

POMEGRANATE • BOX 808022 • PETALUMA, CA 94975

IRELAND 1900
Guinness's Wharf, Dublin

POMEGRANATE • BOX 808022 • PETALUMA, CA 94975

CIRCUS

IRELAND 1900
County Offaly. A circus is set up for business at Rahan, near the Claddiagh River.

POMEGRANATE • BOX 808022 • PETALUMA, CA 94975

IRELAND 1900
Donegal City at the head of Donegal Bay

POMEGRANATE • BOX 808022 • PETALUMA, CA 94975

IRELAND 1900
St. Stephen's Green, Dublin

POMEGRANATE • BOX 808022 • PETALUMA, CA 94975

IRELAND 1900
County Antrim. Haymaking at Red Bay

POMEGRANATE • BOX 808022 • PETALUMA, CA 94975

CORK. SHANDON & BLACKPOOL. 494.

IRELAND 1900
The city of Cork

POMEGRANATE • BOX 808022 • PETALUMA, CA 94975

O'Connell Street and Bridge, Dublin.

IRELAND 1900
O'Connell Street, Dublin. This picture was taken from the O'Connell Bridge, which spans the River Liffey.

POMEGRANATE • BOX 808022 • PETALUMA, CA 94975

IRELAND 1900
County Roscommon. A milkman makes his rounds.

POMEGRANATE • BOX 808022 • PETALUMA, CA 94975

IRELAND 1900

County Galway. The statue of Padraig O'Conaire (1882–1923), a renowned Galway-born story-teller, is located in Eyre Square Park in Galway.

POMEGRANATE • BOX 808022 • PETALUMA, CA 94975

ZILLAH
LIVERPOOL

IRELAND 1900

The Customs House, Dublin. Completed in 1791 on the design of London-born architect James Gandon, this building is a fine example of the Georgian period of architecture in Dublin. The River Liffey is in the foreground.

POMEGRANATE • BOX 808022 • PETALUMA, CA 94975

IRELAND 1900
The city of Limerick located on the River Shannon

POMEGRANATE • BOX 808022 • PETALUMA, CA 94975

IRELAND 1900

A typical blackthorn seller. Branches from the blackthorn tree are said to make the best walking-sticks in the world.

POMEGRANATE • BOX 808022 • PETALUMA, CA 94975

BALLYSHANNON FALLS. 4698. W.L.

IRELAND 1900

Ballyshannon Falls. Ballyshannon is a port located where the Erne enters Donegal Bay, noted especially for its salmon fishing.

POMEGRANATE • BOX 808022 • PETALUMA, CA 94975

SWANTON
SWAIN

IRELAND 1900
County Cork. The horse fair at Bantry

POMEGRANATE • BOX 808022 • PETALUMA, CA 94975

IRELAND 1900
Turf cutting in Connemara

POMEGRANATE • BOX 808022 • PETALUMA, CA 94975

W: YOUNGER & Co

IRELAND 1900

St. Patrick's Bridge and quay at the River Lee, Cork

POMEGRANATE • BOX 808022 • PETALUMA, CA 94975

Tylers'
BOOTS
ARE THE BEST
BRANCHES
EVERYWHERE
HATCH ST
QUEEN

IRELAND 1900
Sackville Street, Dublin, before it was named
O'Connell Street

POMEGRANATE • BOX 808022 • PETALUMA, CA 94975

IRELAND 1900
A peasant woman works at her spinning wheel in the doorway of her home.

POMEGRANATE • BOX 808022 • PETALUMA, CA 94975

IRELAND 1900
Dun Laoghaire, formerly known as Kingstown. This harbor was built in the early 19th century to accomodate the mail boat.

POMEGRANATE • BOX 808022 • PETALUMA, CA 94975

IRELAND 1900
Peasants on the Aran Islands, off the coast of Galway

POMEGRANATE • BOX 808022 • PETALUMA, CA 94975

PHILCO
CELTIC

IRELAND 1900
O'Connell Street, the city of Limerick. Limerick was founded by the Danes in the 9th century.

POMEGRANATE • BOX 808022 • PETALUMA, CA 94975

POSTING ESTABLISHMENT

IRELAND 1900
An old farmer of Galway

POMEGRANATE • BOX 808022 • PETALUMA, CA 94975

9
DONNELLY'S
BACON
GRAND
CINEMA
LADIES

IRELAND 1900

O'Connell Street, Dublin, c. 1925, featuring a memorial statue to Daniel O'Connell (1775–1847), the famous political leader who secured Catholic Emancipation in 1829. Behind it rises Nelson's Pillar, a tribute to the British naval hero, Horatio Nelson (1758–1805).

POMEGRANATE • BOX 808022 • PETALUMA, CA 94975

IRELAND 1900

Sackville Street (before it was named O'Connell Street), Dublin, with a view of the General Post Office (built from 1814–18). Nelson's pillar stands in front of the post office.

POMEGRANATE • BOX 808022 • PETALUMA, CA 94975